At Sylvan, we believe that a lifelong love of learning begins at an early age, and we are glad you have chosen our resources to help your children experience the joy of mathematics as they build critical reasoning skills. We know that the time you spend with your children reinforcing the lessons learned in school will contribute to their love of learning.

Success in math requires more than just memorizing basic facts and algorithms; it also requires children to make sense of size, shape, and numbers as they appear in the world. Children who can connect their understanding of math to the world around them will be ready for the challenges of mathematics as they advance to more complex topics.

We use a research-based, step-by-step process in teaching math at Sylvan that includes thought-provoking math problems and activities. As students increase their success as problem solvers, they become more confident. With increasing confidence, students build even more success. The design of the Sylvan workbooks will help you to help your children build the skills and confidence that will contribute to success in school.

Included with your purchase of this workbook is a coupon for a discount at a participating Sylvan center. We hope you will use this coupon to further your children's academic journeys. Let us partner with you to support the development of confident, well-prepared, independent learners.

The Sylvan Team

2nd Grade
Basic Math Success

Published in the United States by Random House, Inc., New York, and in Canada by Random House of Canada Limited, Toronto.

www.tutoring.sylvanlearning.com

Created by Smarterville Productions LLC
Producer & Editorial Direction: The Linguistic Edge
Producer: TJ Trochlil McGreevy
Writer: Amy Kraft
Cover and Interior Illustrations: Shawn Finley and Duendes del Sur
Layout and Art Direction: SunDried Penguin
Director of Product Development: Russell Ginns

First Edition

ISBN: 978-0-375-43036-7

Library of Congress Cataloging-in-Publication Data available upon request.

This book is available at special discounts for bulk purchases for sales promotions or premiums. For more information, write to Special Markets/Premium Sales, 1745 Broadway, MD 6-2, New York, New York 10019 or e-mail specialmarkets@randomhouse.com.

PRINTED IN CHINA

10 9 8 7 6 5 4 3 2 1

Contents

Place Value

Get in Place

WRITE how many tens and ones you see. Then WRITE the number they make.

1.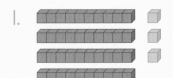

Tens	Ones
5	3

= 53

2.

Tens	Ones

=

3.

Tens	Ones

=

4.

Tens	Ones

=

5.

Tens	Ones

=

6.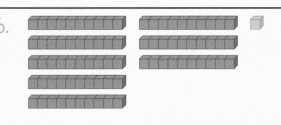

Tens	Ones

=

7.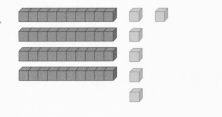

Tens	Ones

=

8.

Tens	Ones

=

Get in Place

  = 10¢    = 1¢

WRITE how many tens and ones you see.
Then WRITE the number they make.

1.

Tens	Ones

=

2.

Tens	Ones

=

3.

Tens	Ones

=

4.

Tens	Ones

=

5.

Tens	Ones

=

6.

Tens	Ones

=

7.

Tens	Ones

=

8.

Tens	Ones

=

Place Value

Get in Place

WRITE how many hundreds, tens, and ones you see. Then WRITE the number they make.

1.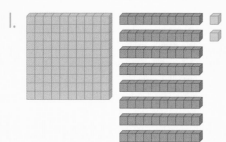

Hundreds	Tens	Ones

=

2.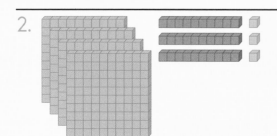

Hundreds	Tens	Ones

=

3.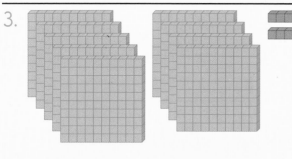

Hundreds	Tens	Ones

=

4.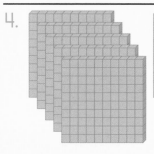

Hundreds	Tens	Ones

=

5.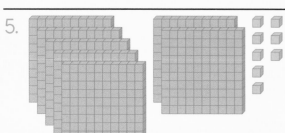

Hundreds	Tens	Ones

=

Number Match

CIRCLE the picture in each row that matches the number.

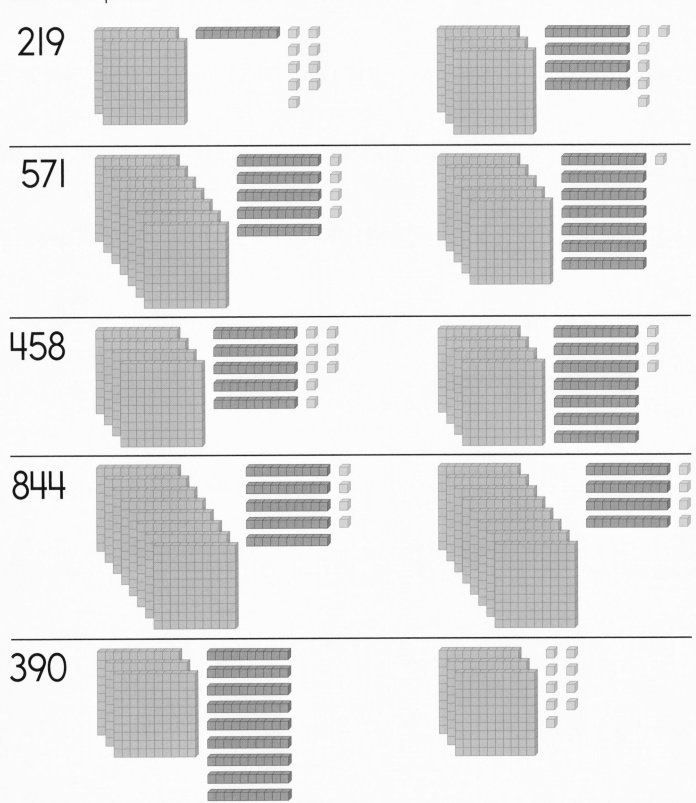

219

571

458

844

390

Write the Number

WRITE the number words.

HINT: Remember to put a hyphen in numbers connecting the tens and ones, like seventy-four or thirty-three.

1 one	11 eleven	30 thirty
2 two	12 twelve	40 forty
3 three	13 thirteen	50 fifty
4 four	14 fourteen	60 sixty
5 five	15 fifteen	70 seventy
6 six	16 sixteen	80 eighty
7 seven	17 seventeen	90 ninety
8 eight	18 eighteen	100 one hundred
9 nine	19 nineteen	
10 ten	20 twenty	

1. 162   one hundred sixty-two

2. 374   _____

3. 250   _____

4. 816   _____

5. 643   _____

6. 495   _____

Match Up

DRAW lines to connect the numbers and words that go together.

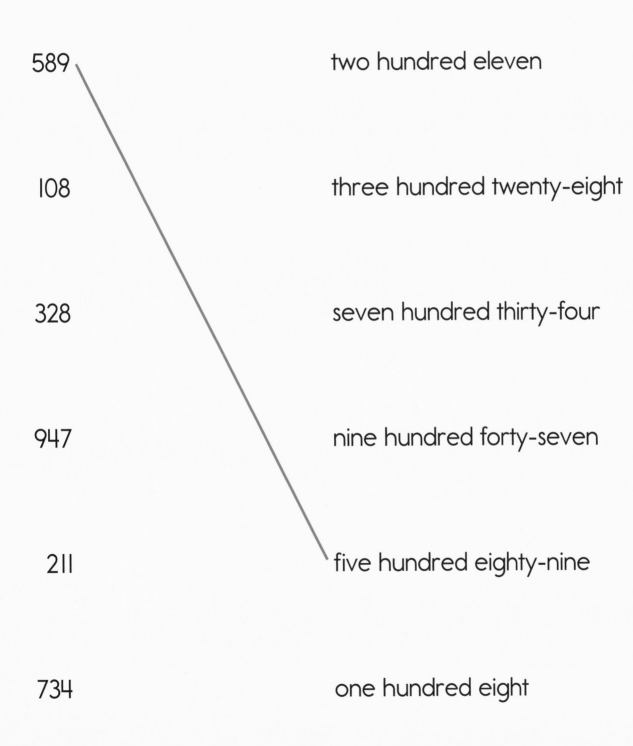

589   two hundred eleven

108   three hundred twenty-eight

328   seven hundred thirty-four

947   nine hundred forty-seven

211   five hundred eighty-nine

734   one hundred eight

Holey Hundreds!

WRITE the missing numbers on the chart. Then COLOR the chart by following the directions on the next page.

1	2		4	5	6	7	8		10
	12	13	14		16	17	18	19	20
21	22	23		25	26		28	29	30
31	32	33	34	35		37	38	39	40
41		43	44	45	46	47	48	49	50
51	52	53	54		56	57	58		60
	62	63	64	65	66	67	68	69	
71	72	73		75	76		78	79	80
81	82	83	84	85	86	87	88	89	90
91		93	94	95	96	97		99	100

1. COLOR number 33 blue.
2. COLOR number 57 red.
3. COLOR number 94 purple.
4. COLOR number 52 orange.

5. COLOR the number that is 2 more than 7 blue.
6. COLOR the number that is 8 more than 17 red.
7. COLOR the number that is 10 less than 71 purple.
8. COLOR the number that is 16 less than 56 orange.

9. Starting at number 8, SKIP COUNT by 10 and COLOR the squares yellow.
10. Starting at number 75, SKIP COUNT by 5 and COLOR the squares green.

1	2		4	5	6	7	8		10
	12	13	14		16	17	18	19	20
21	22	23		25	26		28	29	30
31	3?		34	35		37	38	39	40
41		43	44	45	46	47	48	49	50
51	5?	53	54		56	57	58		60
	62	63	64	65	66	67	68	69	
71	72	73		75	76		78	79	80
81	82	83	84	85	86	87	88	89	90
91		93	94	95	96	97		99	100

Number Lines & Patterns

Pattern Patch

WRITE the missing numbers in the boxes.

82	83	84		86	87		89

103			106	107		109	

	344	345		347			350

719	720						

566							573

						856	857

Get in Line

WRITE the missing numbers on each number line.

234 235 236 237   239 240

      982 983   986   988

97   101   103

874 875

699   706

401 402

Number Lines & Patterns

Get in Line

SKIP COUNT and WRITE the missing numbers on each number line.

Skip count by 2:

2   4   6   8

Skip count by 5:

50   55   60

Skip count by 10:

60   70   80

Skip count by 3:

15   18   21

Skip count by 8:

8   16   24

Skip count by 6:

42   48   54

Pattern Patch

DETERMINE what number is being used for skip counting. Then WRITE the rest of the pattern.

66	68	70					

20	30	40					

15	20	25					

27	30	33					

62	66	70					

42	49	56					

Comparing Numbers

Which One?

CIRCLE the picture in each pair that has **more** than the other.

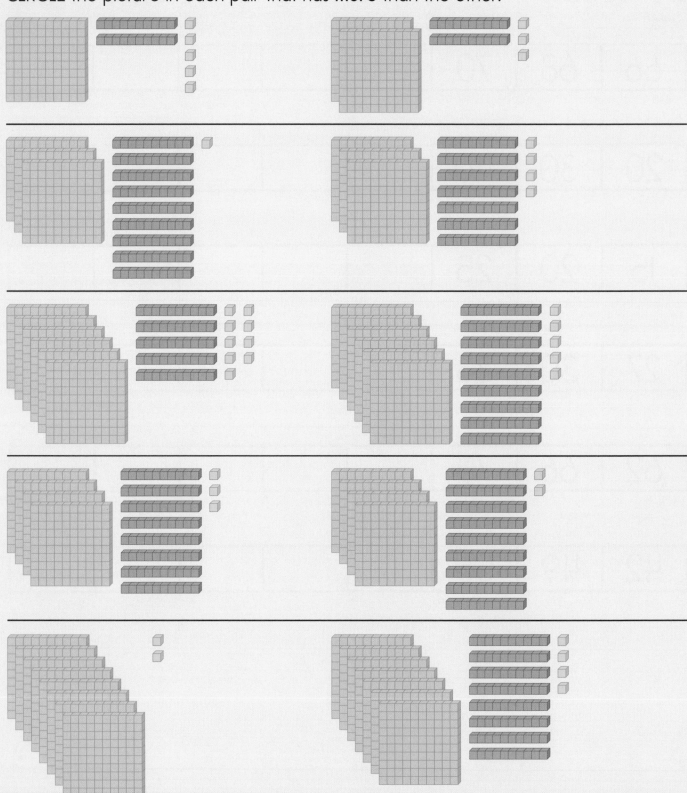

Circle It

CIRCLE the number that is **less** than the number shown in the picture.

1.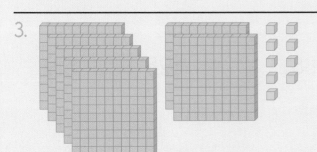

(576)   600

2.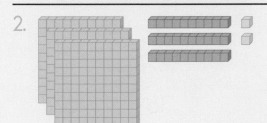

329   340

3.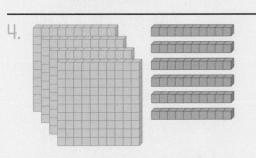

713   707

4.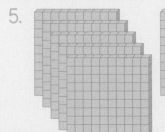

458   464

5.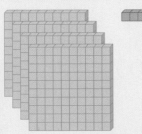

915   910

Comparing Numbers

Mismatched

WRITE > or < in each box.

3 : 8 First, draw two dots next to the larger number.

3 · : 8 Next, draw one dot next to the smaller number.

3 < 8 Then, connect the dots.

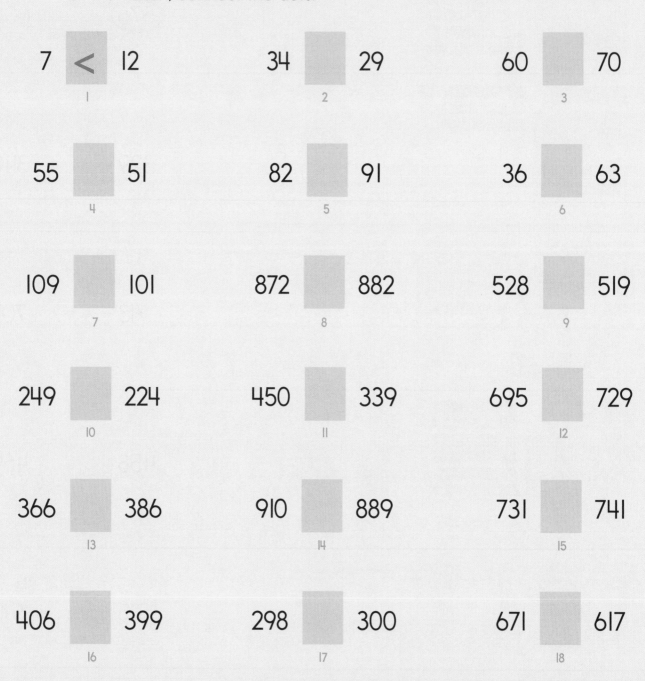

7 < 12   1

34 ☐ 29   2

60 ☐ 70   3

55 ☐ 51   4

82 ☐ 91   5

36 ☐ 63   6

109 ☐ 101   7

872 ☐ 882   8

528 ☐ 519   9

249 ☐ 224   10

450 ☐ 339   11

695 ☐ 729   12

366 ☐ 386   13

910 ☐ 889   14

731 ☐ 741   15

406 ☐ 399   16

298 ☐ 300   17

671 ☐ 617   18

Matched or Mismatched?

WRITE >, <, or = in each box.

HINT: Use = when numbers are the same.

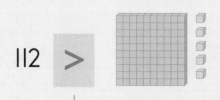

112 ⟩   1

247   2

735   3

490   4

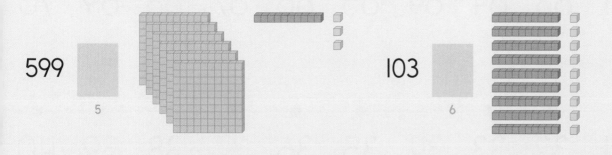

599   5

103   6

381   7

227   8

Rounding & Estimating

Round About

Rounding makes numbers easier to use.

Numbers that end in 1 through 4 get rounded **down** to the nearest ten.

Numbers that end in 5 through 9 get rounded **up** to the nearest ten.

20 21 22 23 24 25 26 27 28 29 30

20   30

ROUND each red number to the nearest ten.

10 11 12 13 14 15 16 17 18 19 20

1   2

60 61 63 64 64 65 66 67 68 69 70

3   4

30 31 32 33 34 35 36 37 38 39 40

5   6

50 51 52 53 54 55 56 57 58 59 60

7   8

Round About

Numbers that end in 1 through 49 get rounded **down** to the nearest hundred.

Numbers that end in 50 through 99 get rounded **up** to the nearest hundred.

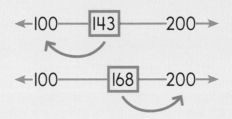

ROUND each number to the nearest hundred.

1. 689

2. 906

3. 415

4. 279

5. 538

6. 391

7. 155

8. 748

9. 332

10. 873

11. 650

12. 942

Rounding & Estimating

Guess and Check

Estimating is making a reasonable guess about something. GUESS the number of cubes in each set, then CHECK your guess by counting the cubes.

1.

Guess:

Check:

2.

Guess:

Check:

3.

Guess:

Check:

Loop It

GUESS the number of bugs. Then CIRCLE groups of five to count the bugs and check your guess.

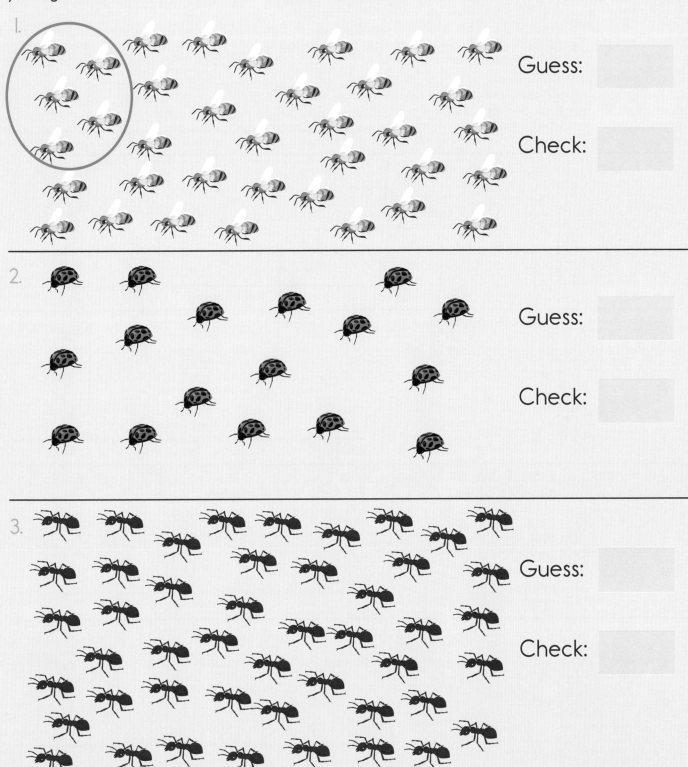

1.

Guess:

Check:

2.

Guess:

Check:

3.

Guess:

Check:

Write the Number

WRITE the number and the number words for each picture.

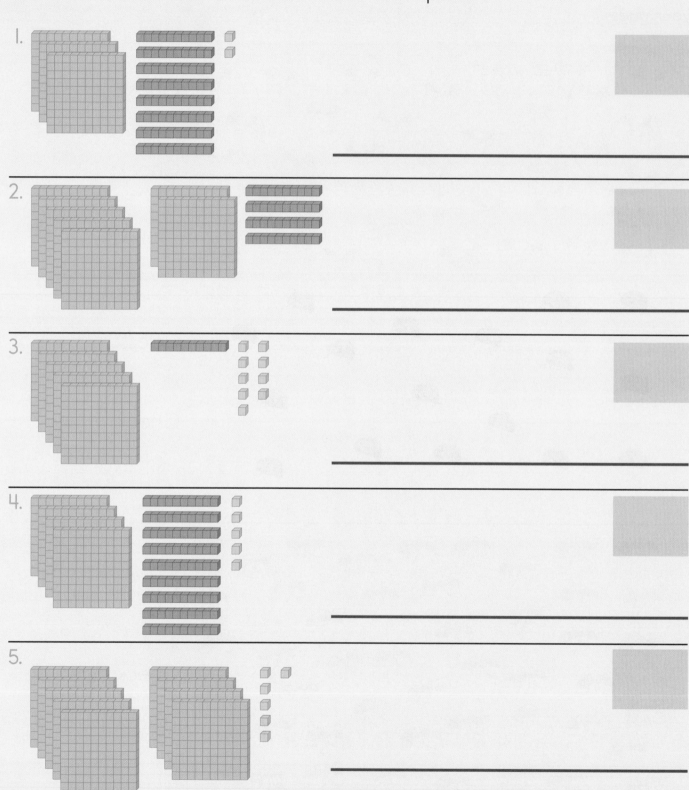

1.

_____

2.

_____

3.

_____

4.

_____

5.

_____

Get in Line

WRITE the missing numbers on each number line.

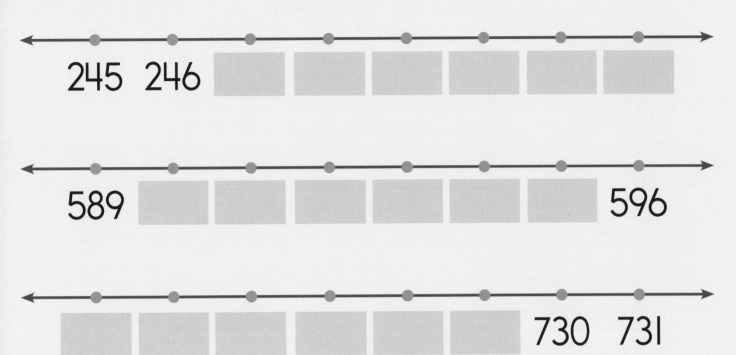

245 246

589   596

730 731

WRITE the missing numbers to finish each pattern.

40	45	50					

26	29	32					

11	17	23					

Matched or Mismatched?

WRITE >, <, or = in each box.

1.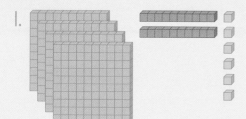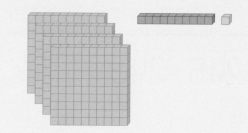

2.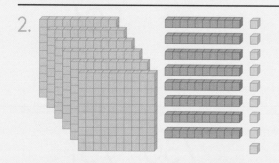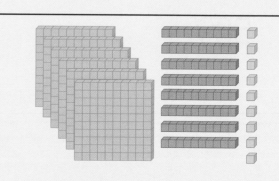

3.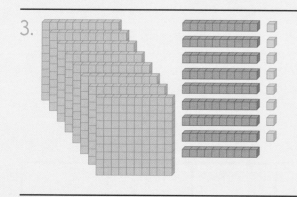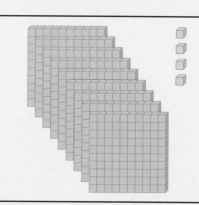

4. 588 577   5. 120 135   6. 311 311

7. 271 274   8. 999 989   9. 759 763

Round About

ROUND each number to the nearest ten.

88
1

31
2

44
3

57
4

12
5

95
6

7
7

15
8

ROUND each number to the nearest hundred.

604
9

178
10

497
11

739
12

218
13

360
14

852
15

243
16

Guess and Check

GUESS the number of jellybeans. Then CIRCLE groups of five to count the jellybeans and check your guess.

Guess:

Check:
17

25

Adding

Picture It

WRITE each sum.

$$52$$
$$+ \, 34$$
$$\overline{86}$$ 8 tens, 6 ones

1. $$31$$
   $$+ \, 25$$

2. $$17$$
   $$+ \, 12$$

3. $$11$$
   $$+ \, 67$$

4. $$24$$
   $$+ \, 20$$

5. $$46$$
   $$+ \, 22$$

6. $$33$$
   $$+ \, 36$$

Cash Crunch

WRITE each sum.

1.

   21¢   +   41¢   =   ☐ ¢

2.

   81¢   +   15¢   =   ☐ ¢

3.

   23¢   +   21¢   =   ☐ ¢

4.

   57¢   +   32¢   =   ☐ ¢

5.

   33¢   +   24¢   =   ☐ ¢

6.

   27¢   +   52¢   =   ☐ ¢

Adding

It All Adds Up

WRITE each sum.

1.
$$\begin{array}{r} 62 \\ + 17 \\ \hline \end{array}$$

2.
$$\begin{array}{r} 13 \\ + 41 \\ \hline \end{array}$$

3.
$$\begin{array}{r} 88 \\ + 10 \\ \hline \end{array}$$

4.
$$\begin{array}{r} 55 \\ + 32 \\ \hline \end{array}$$

5.
$$\begin{array}{r} 22 \\ + 22 \\ \hline \end{array}$$

6.
$$\begin{array}{r} 20 \\ + 19 \\ \hline \end{array}$$

7.
$$\begin{array}{r} 64 \\ + 12 \\ \hline \end{array}$$

8.
$$\begin{array}{r} 43 \\ + 26 \\ \hline \end{array}$$

9. 44 + 33 =

10. 30 + 18 =

11. 10 + 21 =

12. 25 + 72 =

13. 18 + 41 =

14. 80 + 14 =

15. 32 + 32 =

16. 54 + 35 =

It All Adds Up

WRITE each missing number.

1.
$$
\begin{array}{r}
65 \\
+ \boxed{} \\
\hline
75
\end{array}
$$

2.
$$
\begin{array}{r}
38 \\
+ \boxed{} \\
\hline
59
\end{array}
$$

3.
$$
\begin{array}{r}
14 \\
+ \boxed{} \\
\hline
26
\end{array}
$$

4.
$$
\begin{array}{r}
53 \\
+ \boxed{} \\
\hline
98
\end{array}
$$

5.
$$
\begin{array}{r}
41 \\
+ \boxed{} \\
\hline
83
\end{array}
$$

6.
$$
\begin{array}{r}
11 \\
+ \boxed{} \\
\hline
76
\end{array}
$$

7.
$$
\begin{array}{r}
25 \\
+ \boxed{} \\
\hline
97
\end{array}
$$

8.
$$
\begin{array}{r}
70 \\
+ \boxed{} \\
\hline
88
\end{array}
$$

9. $\boxed{} + 77 = 99$

10. $50 + \boxed{} = 63$

11. $31 + \boxed{} = 82$

12. $\boxed{} + 16 = 59$

13. $\boxed{} + 40 = 72$

14. $64 + \boxed{} = 95$

15. $12 + \boxed{} = 34$

16. $\boxed{} + 81 = 93$

Subtracting

Picture It

WRITE each difference.

$$37$$
$$-\ 12$$
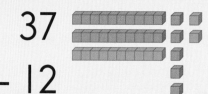

$$25 \quad \text{2 tens, 5 ones}$$

1. $$74$$
   $$-\ 31$$
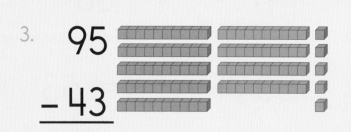

2. $$58$$
   $$-\ 26$$
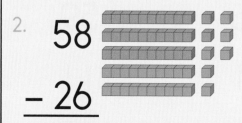

3. $$95$$
   $$-\ 43$$

4. $$89$$
   $$-\ 64$$
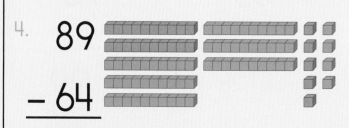

5. $$35$$
   $$-\ 22$$

6. $$77$$
   $$-\ 16$$
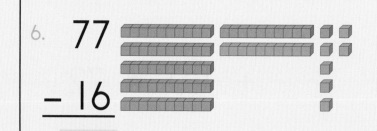

Cash Crunch

WRITE each difference.

HINT: Cross out dimes and pennies to help you subtract.

1.

   48¢   –   13¢   =   35 ¢

2.

   64¢   –   33¢   =   ¢

3.

   81¢   –   21¢   =   ¢

4.

   38¢   –   26¢   =   ¢

5.

   99¢   –   73¢   =   ¢

6.

   83¢   –   42¢   =   ¢

Subtracting

What's the Difference?

WRITE each difference.

1. $\begin{array}{r} 59 \\ -32 \\ \hline \end{array}$

2. $\begin{array}{r} 36 \\ -26 \\ \hline \end{array}$

3. $\begin{array}{r} 62 \\ -41 \\ \hline \end{array}$

4. $\begin{array}{r} 87 \\ -75 \\ \hline \end{array}$

5. $\begin{array}{r} 91 \\ -10 \\ \hline \end{array}$

6. $\begin{array}{r} 48 \\ -23 \\ \hline \end{array}$

7. $\begin{array}{r} 76 \\ -14 \\ \hline \end{array}$

8. $\begin{array}{r} 58 \\ -45 \\ \hline \end{array}$

9. $60 - 20 =$

10. $39 - 28 =$

11. $46 - 16 =$

12. $55 - 31 =$

13. $73 - 21 =$

14. $28 - 13 =$

15. $95 - 23 =$

16. $88 - 57 =$

6

What's the Difference?

WRITE each missing number.

1. $$\begin{array}{r} 90 \\ -\ \boxed{} \\ \hline 40 \end{array}$$

2. $$\begin{array}{r} 79 \\ -\ \boxed{} \\ \hline 33 \end{array}$$

3. $$\begin{array}{r} 24 \\ -\ \boxed{} \\ \hline 12 \end{array}$$

4. $$\begin{array}{r} 56 \\ -\ \boxed{} \\ \hline 41 \end{array}$$

5. $$\begin{array}{r} 63 \\ -\ \boxed{} \\ \hline 22 \end{array}$$

6. $$\begin{array}{r} 85 \\ -\ \boxed{} \\ \hline 65 \end{array}$$

7. $$\begin{array}{r} 37 \\ -\ \boxed{} \\ \hline 10 \end{array}$$

8. $$\begin{array}{r} 92 \\ -\ \boxed{} \\ \hline 71 \end{array}$$

9. $\boxed{} - 23 = 72$

10. $45 - \boxed{} = 11$

11. $83 - \boxed{} = 53$

12. $\boxed{} - 19 = 50$

13. $\boxed{} - 11 = 64$

14. $68 - \boxed{} = 44$

15. $78 - \boxed{} = 21$

16. $\boxed{} - 32 = 16$

Adding with Regrouping

Picture It

WRITE each sum.

26

+ 45

6 tens, 11 ones

71 7 tens, 1 one

11 ones = 1 ten, 1 one

1. 19
    + 23

2. 56
    + 37

3. 48
    + 34

4. 36
    + 29

5. 78
    + 13

6. 53
    + 17

Cash Crunch

WRITE each sum.

HINT: Remember that the value of ten pennies equals one dime.

1.   16¢   +   49¢   =   ___ ¢

2.   74¢   +   18¢   =   ___ ¢

3.   29¢   +   41¢   =   ___ ¢

4.   35¢   +   46¢   =   ___ ¢

5.   25¢   +   27¢   =   ___ ¢

6.   58¢   +   15¢   =   ___ ¢

Adding with Regrouping

It All Adds Up

WRITE each sum.

$\begin{array}{r} 29 \\ +13 \\ \hline \end{array}$	First, add the numbers in the ones place. 9 + 3 = 12	$\begin{array}{r} {\scriptstyle 1} \\ 29 \\ +13 \\ \hline 2 \end{array}$	Write a 2 in the ones place, and write a 1 in the tens place.	$\begin{array}{r} {\scriptstyle 1} \\ 29 \\ +13 \\ \hline 42 \end{array}$	Then add the tens. 1 + 2 + 1 = 4. Write 4 in the tens place. 29 + 13 = 42

1. $\begin{array}{r} 26 \\ +35 \\ \hline \end{array}$

2. $\begin{array}{r} 62 \\ +19 \\ \hline \end{array}$

3. $\begin{array}{r} 75 \\ +15 \\ \hline \end{array}$

4. $\begin{array}{r} 37 \\ +54 \\ \hline \end{array}$

5. $\begin{array}{r} 48 \\ +22 \\ \hline \end{array}$

6. $\begin{array}{r} 37 \\ +37 \\ \hline \end{array}$

7. $\begin{array}{r} 17 \\ +18 \\ \hline \end{array}$

8. $\begin{array}{r} 39 \\ +19 \\ \hline \end{array}$

9. $\begin{array}{r} 16 \\ +16 \\ \hline \end{array}$

10. $\begin{array}{r} 66 \\ +14 \\ \hline \end{array}$

11. $\begin{array}{r} 28 \\ +38 \\ \hline \end{array}$

12. $\begin{array}{r} 58 \\ +34 \\ \hline \end{array}$

It All Adds Up

WRITE each sum.

1. 47 + 13 =

2. 18 + 57 =

3. 24 + 68 =

4. 48 + 19 =

5. 36 + 54 =

6. 27 + 14 =

7. 49 + 33 =

8. 11 + 39 =

9. 54 + 17 =

10. 35 + 29 =

11. 79 + 21 =

12. 48 + 47 =

Subtracting with Regrouping

Picture It

WRITE each difference.

$$42$$
$$-\ 15$$

$$27\ \text{2 tens, 7 ones}$$

1. 93
   $-\ 26$

2. 70
   $-\ 54$

3. 76
   $-\ 37$

4. 81
   $-\ 8$

5. 66
   $-\ 48$

6. 52
   $-\ 25$

Picture It

WRITE each difference.

HINT: Color the number of cubes being subtracted, then count the number of cubes remaining.

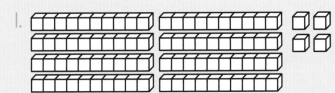

1. $84 - 56 =$

2. $36 - 18 =$

3. $61 - 22 =$

4. $95 - 29 =$

5. $73 - 58 =$

6. $62 - 5 =$

Subtracting with Regrouping

What's the Difference?

WRITE each difference.

53 − 16	First, regroup from the tens place. Cross out the 5 and write 4, and cross out the 3 and write 13.	4 13 5̷3̷ − 16 7	Subtract in the ones place: 13 − 6 = 7. Write 7 in the ones place.	4 13 5̷3̷ − 16 37	Then, subtract in the tens place: 4 − 1 = 3. Write 3 in the tens place. 53 − 16 = 37

1.
$$\begin{array}{r} 78 \\ -\ 19 \\ \hline \end{array}$$

2.
$$\begin{array}{r} 35 \\ -\ 27 \\ \hline \end{array}$$

3.
$$\begin{array}{r} 44 \\ -\ 15 \\ \hline \end{array}$$

4.
$$\begin{array}{r} 30 \\ -\ 12 \\ \hline \end{array}$$

5.
$$\begin{array}{r} 85 \\ -\ 47 \\ \hline \end{array}$$

6.
$$\begin{array}{r} 93 \\ -\ 68 \\ \hline \end{array}$$

7.
$$\begin{array}{r} 82 \\ -\ 56 \\ \hline \end{array}$$

8.
$$\begin{array}{r} 73 \\ -\ 18 \\ \hline \end{array}$$

9.
$$\begin{array}{r} 63 \\ -\ 26 \\ \hline \end{array}$$

10.
$$\begin{array}{r} 95 \\ -\ 86 \\ \hline \end{array}$$

11.
$$\begin{array}{r} 64 \\ -\ 36 \\ \hline \end{array}$$

12.
$$\begin{array}{r} 47 \\ -\ 28 \\ \hline \end{array}$$

8

What's the Difference?

WRITE each difference.

1. 52 – 35 =

2. 61 – 57 =

3. 98 – 19 =

4. 74 – 17 =

5. 47 – 28 =

6. 51 – 13 =

7. 41 – 18 =

8. 80 – 39 =

9. 65 – 26 =

10. 72 – 25 =

11. 90 – 16 =

12. 54 – 45 =

Work It Out

Hector is deciding which two things to buy at the Eddie's Electronics store. He sees a video game for 31 dollars, a DVD for 25 dollars, a game controller for 15 dollars, a pack of batteries for 8 dollars, and headphones for 14 dollars.

WRITE the total cost of each of these possible purchases.

1. A pack of batteries and headphones $ _____

2. A DVD and a game controller $ _____

3. Headphones and a video game $ _____

4. A game controller and a pack of batteries $ _____

5. A video game and a DVD $ _____

6. If Hector has $20 and buys headphones, how much money would he have left? $ _____

Work It Out

Betty and Joe love to eat hamburgers in the summertime. They ate 23 hamburgers in June, 26 hamburgers in July, and 18 hamburgers in August.

1. How many total hamburgers did Betty and Joe eat in June and July? _____

2. How many total hamburgers did they eat in July and August? _____

3. If Joe ate 15 hamburgers in June, how many did Betty eat that month? _____

4. If Betty ate 14 hamburgers in July, how many did Joe eat that month? _____

Unit Rewind

WRITE each missing number.

1. ☐ $+ \ 28 \ = \ 89$

2. $13 \ + \ $ ☐ $\ = \ 54$

3. $45 \ + \ $ ☐ $\ = \ 65$

4. ☐ $+ \ 32 \ = \ 48$

5. ☐ $+ \ 20 \ = \ 99$

6. $61 \ + \ $ ☐ $\ = \ 83$

7. $77 \ - \ $ ☐ $\ = \ 33$

8. ☐ $- \ 16 \ = \ 40$

9. ☐ $- \ 35 \ = \ 54$

10. $97 \ - \ $ ☐ $\ = \ 46$

11. $39 \ - \ $ ☐ $\ = \ 24$

12. ☐ $- \ 15 \ = \ 72$

Unit Rewind

WRITE each sum or difference.

1.
$$\begin{array}{r} 14 \\ + 44 \\ \hline \end{array}$$

2.
$$\begin{array}{r} 28 \\ + 11 \\ \hline \end{array}$$

3.
$$\begin{array}{r} 72 \\ + 23 \\ \hline \end{array}$$

4.
$$\begin{array}{r} 64 \\ + 25 \\ \hline \end{array}$$

5.
$$\begin{array}{r} 39 \\ + 52 \\ \hline \end{array}$$

6.
$$\begin{array}{r} 66 \\ + 15 \\ \hline \end{array}$$

7.
$$\begin{array}{r} 58 \\ + 17 \\ \hline \end{array}$$

8.
$$\begin{array}{r} 37 \\ + 27 \\ \hline \end{array}$$

9.
$$\begin{array}{r} 74 \\ - 32 \\ \hline \end{array}$$

10.
$$\begin{array}{r} 45 \\ - 12 \\ \hline \end{array}$$

11.
$$\begin{array}{r} 99 \\ - 49 \\ \hline \end{array}$$

12.
$$\begin{array}{r} 83 \\ - 62 \\ \hline \end{array}$$

13.
$$\begin{array}{r} 63 \\ - 47 \\ \hline \end{array}$$

14.
$$\begin{array}{r} 30 \\ - 16 \\ \hline \end{array}$$

15.
$$\begin{array}{r} 87 \\ - 39 \\ \hline \end{array}$$

16.
$$\begin{array}{r} 51 \\ - 22 \\ \hline \end{array}$$

Grouping

Pick a Package

How many bags of five marbles can be made from the loose marbles? WRITE the answer.

HINT: Draw circles around groups of five, and count the number of groups you have.

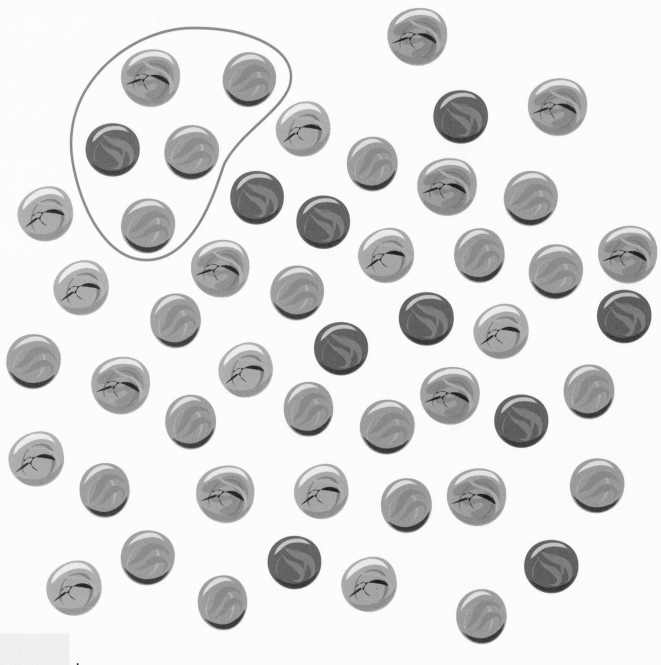

bags

Pick a Package

Each seed packet comes with eight seeds. How many packets are needed to hold the seeds? How many seeds are there? WRITE the answers.

HINT: Draw circles around groups of eight, and use the groups to help you count the seeds.

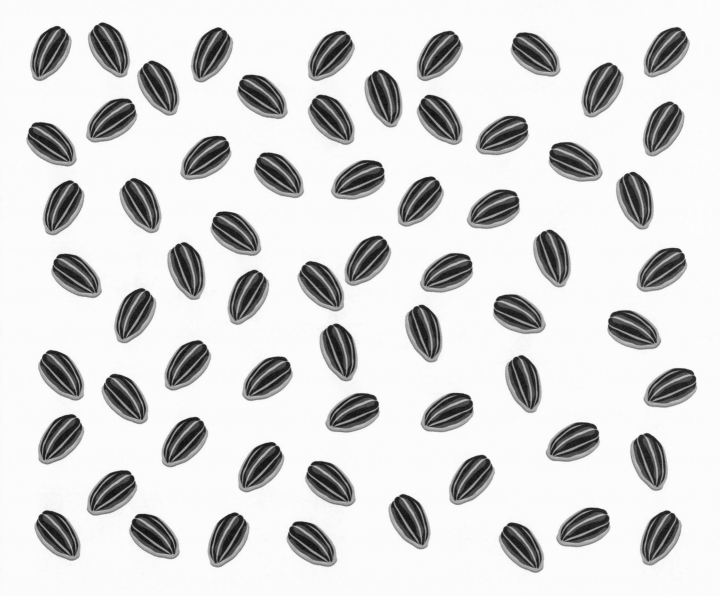

     seed packets for   seeds

Grouping

Pick a Package

How many of each type of box would be needed to pack the chocolates on the conveyor belt? WRITE the answer below each box.

1

2

3

4

Games Galore

WRITE the total number of game parts you see in the four games.

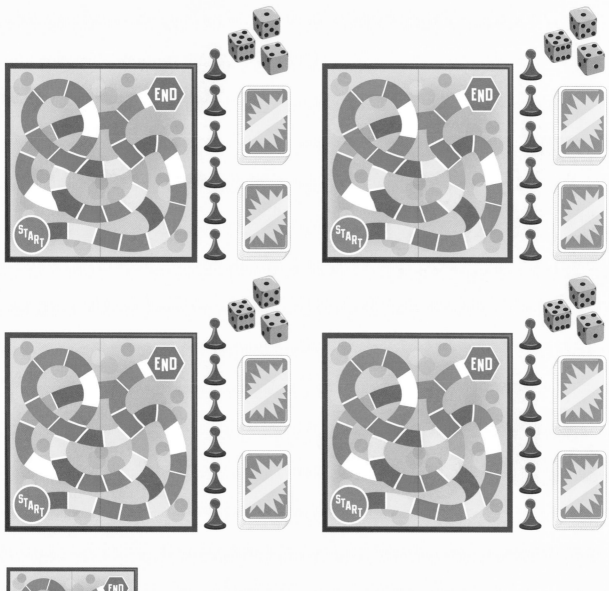

| 1 | 2 | 3 | 4 |

Fair Share

The twins aren't happy unless they get the same number of everything. How many of each treat will they each get? WRITE the answer.

cupcakes

cookies

milk shakes

Fair Share

If the same number of cards is dealt to every player, how many cards will each player get? WRITE the answer.

cards

Fair Share

WRITE the number of gems each pirate will get if they split the treasure equally.

1

2

3

4

Fair Share

A family of five is having dinner, and everyone can eat the same amount of food.
If each type of food is shared equally, how many pieces of each will a person get?
How many pieces will be left over?
WRITE the answers.

1.

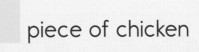 piece of chicken 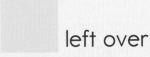 left over

2.

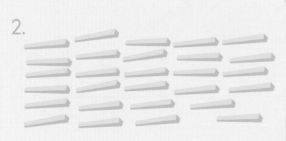

French fries 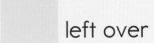 left over

3.

green beans 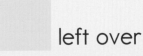 left over

Odd or Even?

An even number of items can be shared equally by two people. An odd number of items cannot be shared equally by two people. There will always be one extra item. CIRCLE **odd** or **even** for each group.

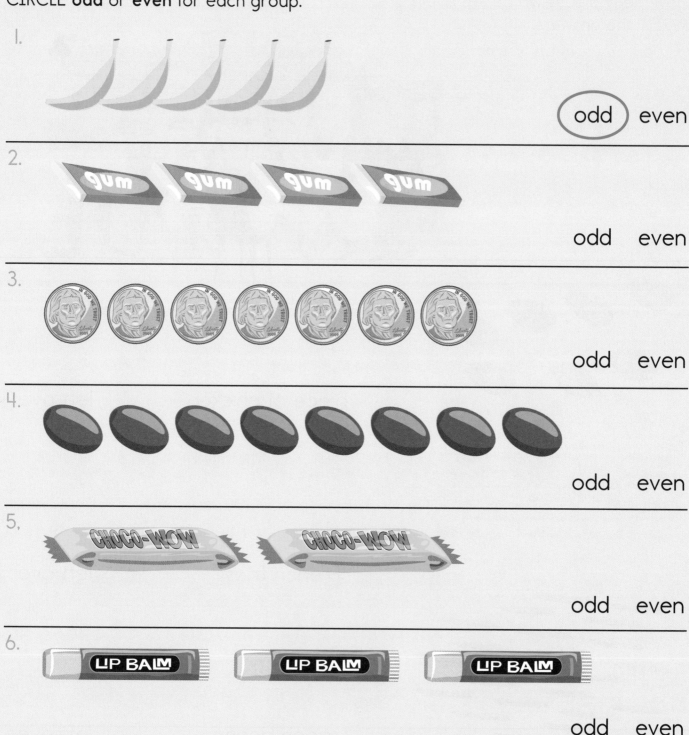

1. (odd) even

2. odd even

3. odd even

4. odd even

5. odd even

6. odd even

Card Tricks

CIRCLE all of the cards with even numbers.

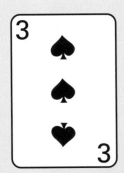  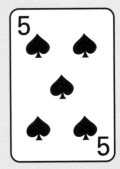

Pick a Package

How many of each bag would be needed to pack all of the candy? WRITE the answer.

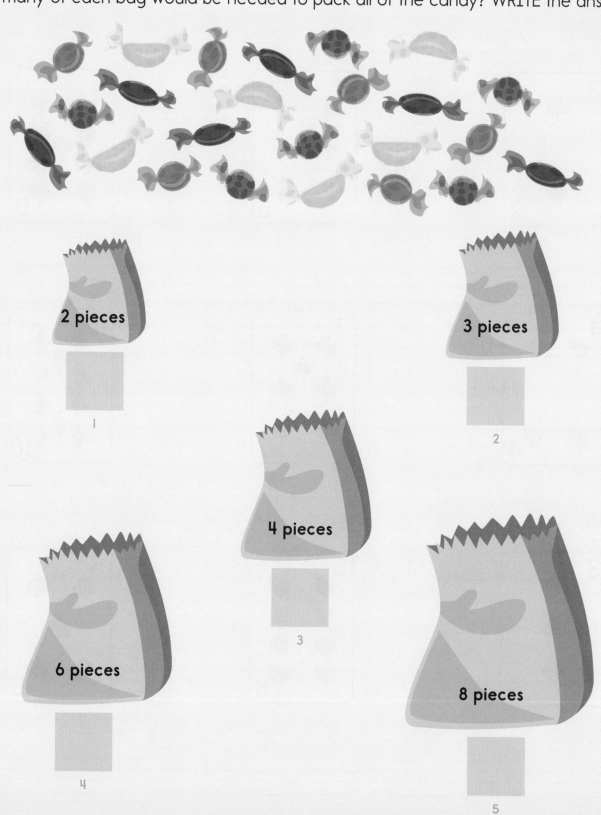

2 pieces

1

3 pieces

2

4 pieces

3

6 pieces

4

8 pieces

5

Fair Share

WRITE the number of bananas each monkey will get when they are shared equally.

1. [   ] bananas

Odd or Even?

CIRCLE **odd** or **even**.

2.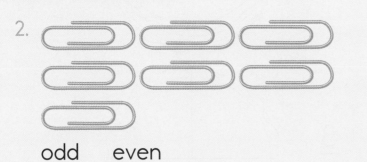

odd   even

3.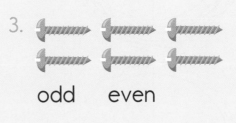

odd   even

4.

odd   even

Piece of Cake

COLOR the cake pieces to match each fraction.

Example:

$\frac{1}{4}$ ← colored piece

← pieces total

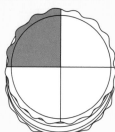

$\frac{1}{2}$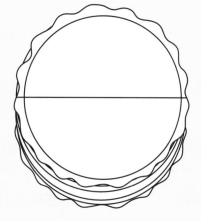

$\frac{1}{3}$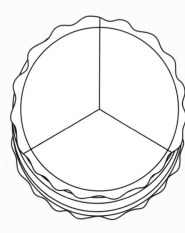

$\frac{2}{4}$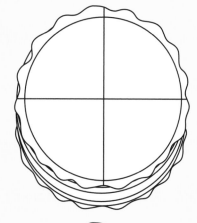

$\frac{2}{2}$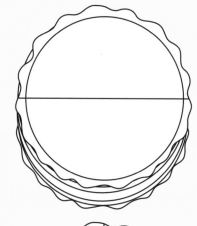

$\frac{2}{3}$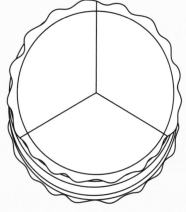

$\frac{3}{4}$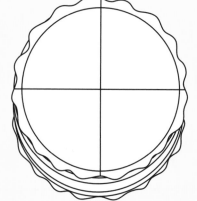

Fraction Bars

WRITE the fraction for each picture.

Example:

$\frac{2}{3}$ ← colored sections

← total sections

1. ———

2. ———

3. ———

4. ———

5. ———

6. ———

Recognizing Fractions

Match Up

DRAW lines to connect the fractions and pictures that go together.

$$\frac{2}{3}$$

$$\frac{1}{4}$$

$$\frac{1}{2}$$

$$\frac{3}{4}$$

$$\frac{1}{3}$$

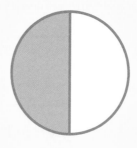
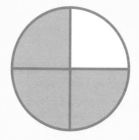

Color the Shapes

COLOR the part or parts of each shape to match the fraction.

$\dfrac{3}{4}$

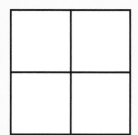

$\dfrac{2}{3}$

$\dfrac{1}{3}$

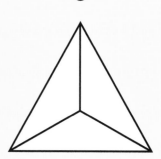

$\dfrac{1}{4}$

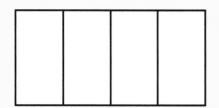

$\dfrac{1}{2}$

$\dfrac{4}{4}$

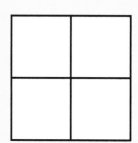

Comparing Fractions

Piece of Cake

COLOR the cake pieces to match each fraction. Then CIRCLE the larger fraction.

HINT: The larger fraction is the one with more of the cake colored.

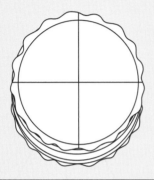 $\dfrac{1}{4}$

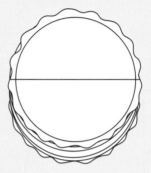 $\dfrac{1}{2}$

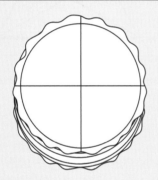 $\dfrac{2}{4}$

 $\dfrac{2}{3}$

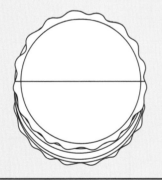 $\dfrac{1}{2}$

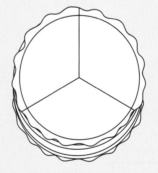 $\dfrac{1}{3}$

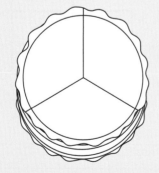 $\dfrac{2}{3}$

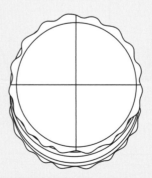 $\dfrac{3}{4}$

Fraction Bars

WRITE the fraction for each picture. Then CIRCLE the smaller fraction.

1.

_____   _____

2.

_____   _____

3.

_____   _____

4.

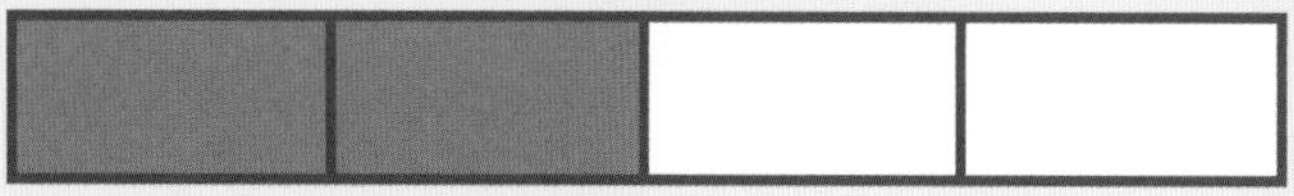

_____   _____

Comparing Fractions

Pizza Party

DRAW a line to match each person to the correct slice of pizza.
Then WRITE answers to the questions.

Alex — I want $\frac{1}{3}$ of a pizza.

Ellie — I want $\frac{3}{4}$ of a pizza.

Kiki — I want $\frac{1}{2}$ of a pizza.

Miles — I want $\frac{1}{4}$ of a pizza.

1. Who has the largest slice of pizza? _____

2. Who has the smallest slice of pizza? _____

Matched or Mismatched?

WRITE >, <, or = in each box.

HINT: Use these fraction circles to help you picture the fractions.

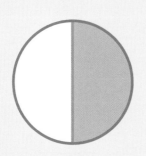 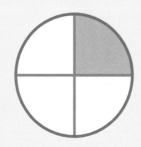 

$\frac{1}{4}$ ☐ $\frac{1}{3}$ $\frac{2}{2}$ ☐ $\frac{2}{3}$ $\frac{2}{4}$ ☐ $\frac{1}{2}$

1   2   3

$\frac{3}{4}$ ☐ $\frac{1}{2}$ $\frac{1}{2}$ ☐ $\frac{1}{3}$ $\frac{3}{3}$ ☐ $\frac{3}{4}$

4   5   6

$\frac{1}{4}$ ☐ $\frac{1}{2}$ $\frac{4}{4}$ ☐ $\frac{3}{3}$ $\frac{1}{2}$ ☐ $\frac{2}{3}$

7   8   9

$\frac{2}{3}$ ☐ $\frac{2}{4}$ $\frac{3}{4}$ ☐ $\frac{1}{3}$ $\frac{2}{3}$ ☐ $\frac{3}{4}$

10   11   12

Match Up

DRAW lines to connect the fractions and pictures that go together.

$$\frac{1}{4}$$

$$\frac{3}{4}$$

$$\frac{2}{3}$$

$$\frac{1}{2}$$

$$\frac{1}{3}$$

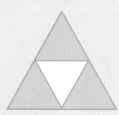

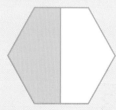

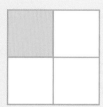

Fraction Bars

COLOR the fraction bars to match each fraction. Then WRITE >, <, or = in each box.

$\frac{1}{3}$ ☐ $\frac{1}{4}$

$\frac{2}{3}$ ☐ $\frac{3}{4}$

$\frac{2}{2}$ ☐ $\frac{4}{4}$

$\frac{1}{2}$ ☐ $\frac{1}{3}$

Nonstandard Units

Measure Up

MEASURE the length of each object in paper clips.

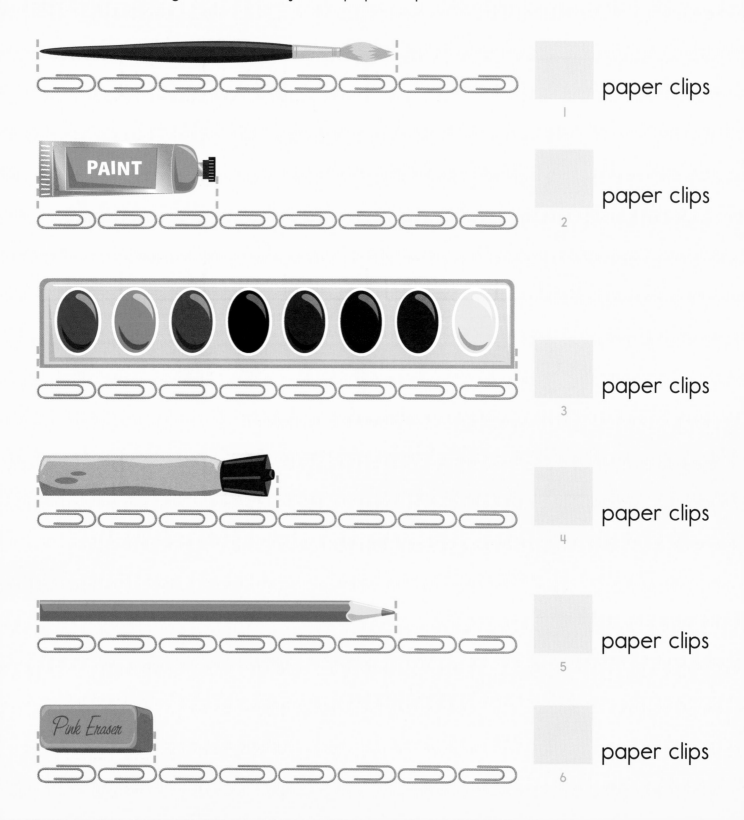

paper clips

paper clips

paper clips

paper clips

paper clips

paper clips

Measure Up

MEASURE the length of each object in dimes.

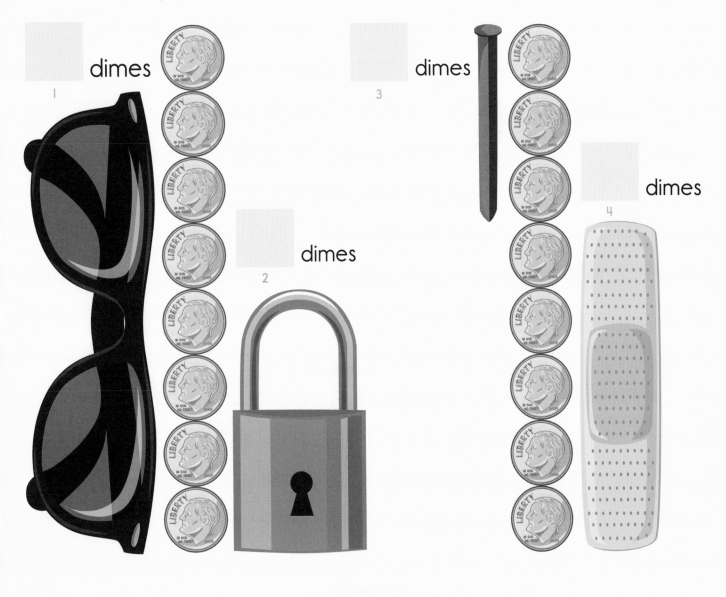

dimes

1

dimes

2

dimes

3

dimes

4

dimes

5

Nonstandard Units

Dime Line

The lizard at the top is 5 dimes long. GUESS the length of each lizard in dimes. Then LINE UP some dimes, and MEASURE each lizard.

1.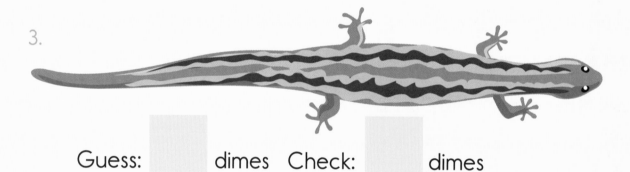

Guess: ___ dimes

Check: ___ dimes

2.

Guess: ___ dimes   Check: ___ dimes

3.

Guess: ___ dimes   Check: ___ dimes

4.

Guess: ___ dimes

Check: ___ dimes

5.

Guess: ___ dimes

Check: ___ dimes

Dime Line

Each piece of yarn needs to be cut to a particular length. First, DRAW a line on each piece, estimating where it will be cut. Then MEASURE using dimes, and DRAW a line in the correct place. How good was your estimate?

5 dimes

estimate   measure

8 dimes

2 dimes

6 dimes

9 dimes

3 dimes

Measure Up

MEASURE the length of each object in inches.

HINT: *Inch* and *inches* are abbreviated as *in.*

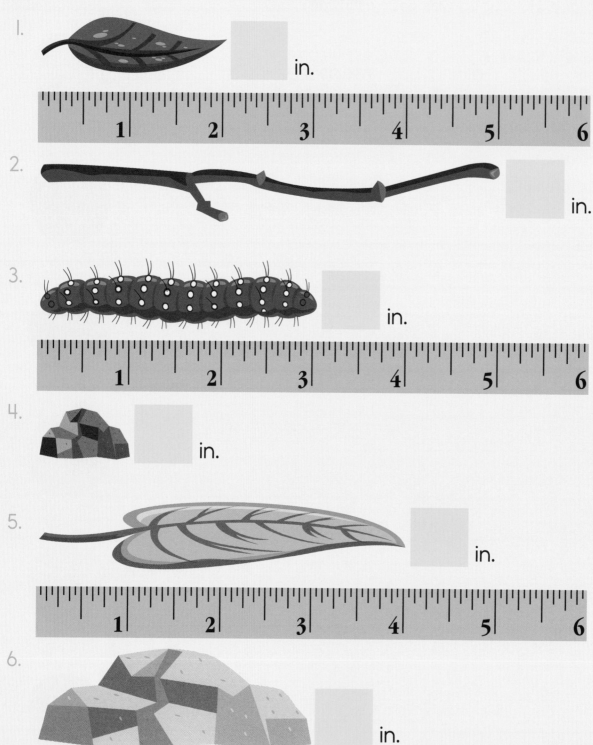

1. [   ] in.

2. [   ] in.

3. [   ] in.

4. [   ] in.

5. [   ] in.

6. [   ] in.

Measure Up

MEASURE the approximate height of each flower in inches.

HINT: To find the approximate height, measure each flower and find the closest number on the ruler.

about [ ] in.

1

about [ ] in.

2

about [ ] in.

3

about [ ] in.

4

Rulers Rule

The candy at the top is 4 inches long. GUESS the length of each piece of candy in inches. Then MEASURE each one with a ruler to check your guess.

1.

Guess: ____ in.   Check: ____ in.

2.

Guess: ____ in.   Check: ____ in.

3.

Guess: ____ in.   Check: ____ in.

4.

Guess: ____ in.   Check: ____ in.

5.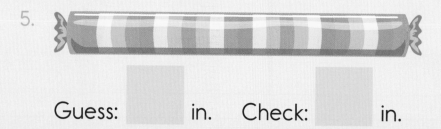

Guess: ____ in.   Check: ____ in.

Rulers Rule

Each piece of yarn needs to be cut to a particular length. First, DRAW a line on each piece, estimating where it will be cut. Then MEASURE with a ruler, and DRAW a line in the correct place. How good was your estimate?

3 in.

1 in.

6 in.

4 in.

2 in.

5 in.

Centimeters

Measure Up

MEASURE the length of each ribbon in centimeters.

HINT: *Centimeter(s)* is abbreviated as *cm*.

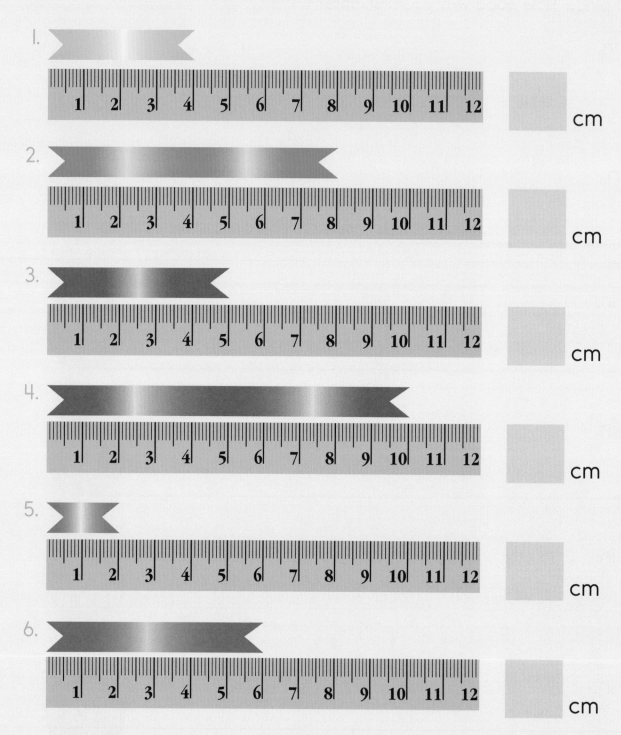

1. ☐ cm

2. ☐ cm

3. ☐ cm

4. ☐ cm

5. ☐ cm

6. ☐ cm

Measure Up

MEASURE the approximate height of each action figure in centimeters.

Centimeters

Rulers Rule

The worm at the top is 10 centimeters long. GUESS the length of each worm in centimeters. Then MEASURE each worm with a ruler to check your guess.

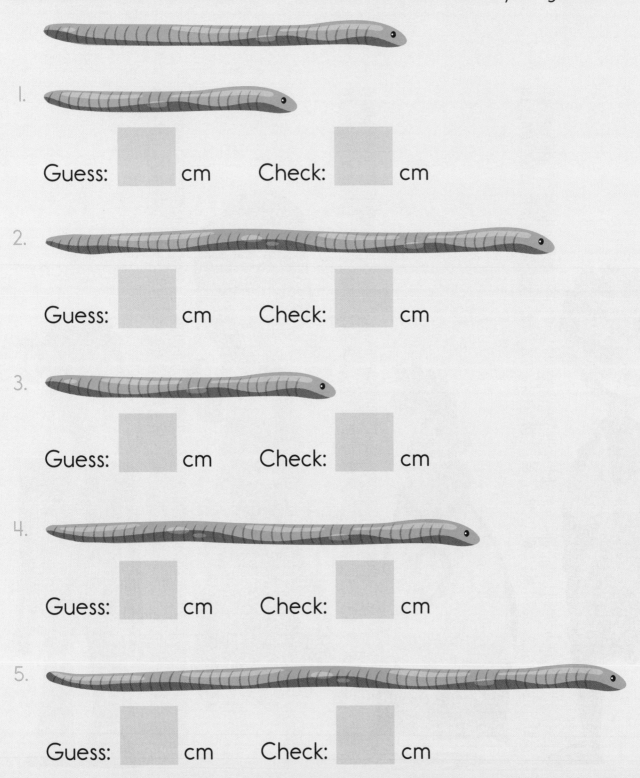

1. Guess: ____ cm   Check: ____ cm

2. Guess: ____ cm   Check: ____ cm

3. Guess: ____ cm   Check: ____ cm

4. Guess: ____ cm   Check: ____ cm

5. Guess: ____ cm   Check: ____ cm

Rulers Rule

Each piece of yarn needs to be cut to a particular length. First, DRAW a line on each piece, estimating where it will be cut. Then MEASURE with a ruler, and DRAW a line in the correct place. How good was your estimate?

6 cm

4 cm

2 cm

9 cm

7 cm

3 cm

Perimeter & Area

Around We Go

Perimeter is the distance around a two-dimensional shape. WRITE the perimeter of each shape.

Example:

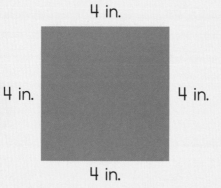

5 in.

3 in.   3 in.

5 in.

To find the perimeter, add the length of all of the sides.

5 + 3 + 5 + 3 = 16

The perimeter of this rectangle is 16 inches.

1.

4 in.

4 in.   4 in.

4 in.

in.

2.

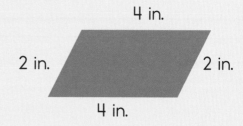

4 in.

2 in.   2 in.

4 in.

in.

3.

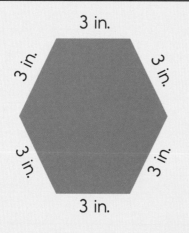

3 in.

3 in.   3 in.

3 in.   3 in.

3 in.

in.

4.

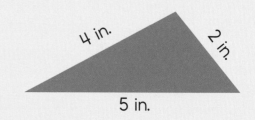

4 in.   2 in.

5 in.

in.

Around We Go

MEASURE the length of each side of the shape in centimeters. Then WRITE the perimeter of the shape.

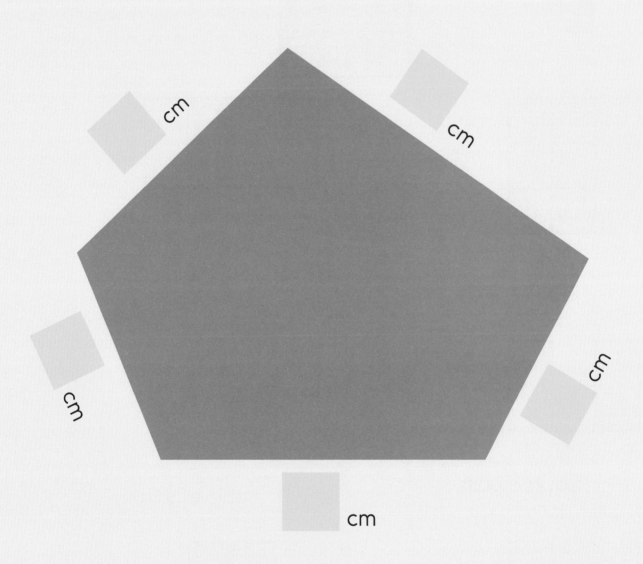

cm

cm

cm

cm

cm

Perimeter: _____ cm

Squared Away

Area is the size of the surface of a shape, and it is measured in square units.
WRITE the area of each shape.

Example: ☐ I square unit

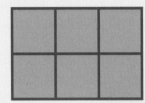 To measure the area, count the number of square units. The area of this rectangle is 6 square units.

1.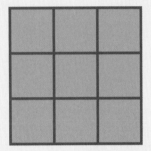

_____ square units

2.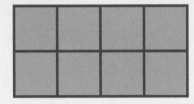

_____ square units

3.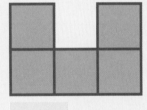

_____ square units

4.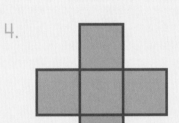

_____ square units

5.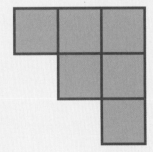

_____ square units

6.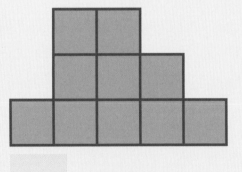

_____ square units

Which One?

CIRCLE the shape that matches each area measurement.

1.

4 square units

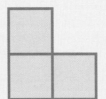 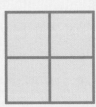

2.

7 square units

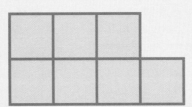 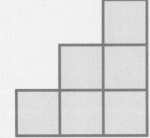

3.

5 square units

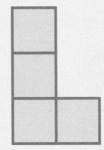 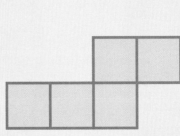

4.

6 square units

 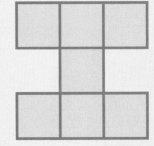

Work It Out

The Scrantonville Scouts just returned from their fishing trip at the lake. Sarah caught a fish that is 5 inches long. Willa caught a fish that is about 4 inches long. Jackie caught a fish measuring over 6 inches.

WRITE the name of each girl above her fish.

2. _____

1. _____

3. _____

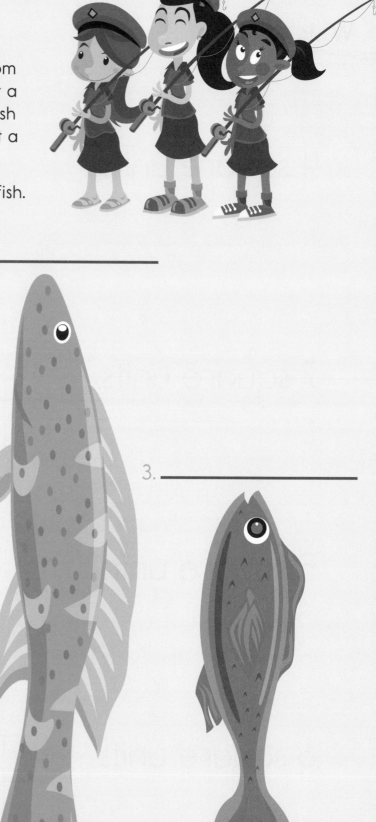

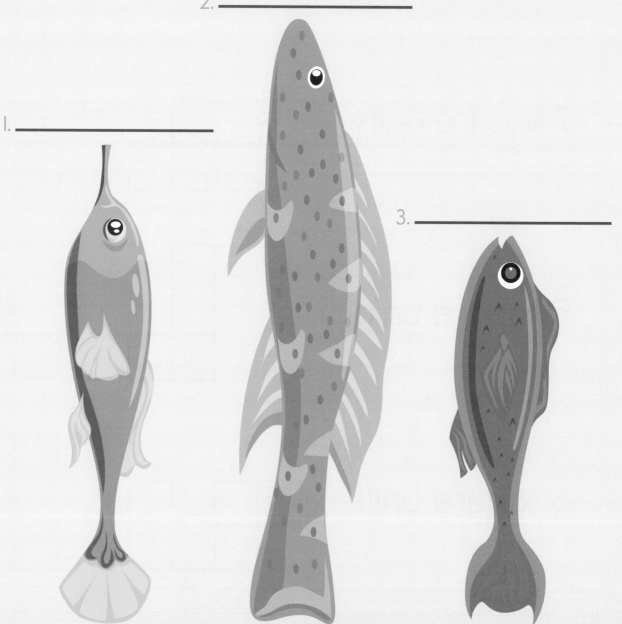

Measure Up

WRITE the approximate length of each object in inches and centimeters.

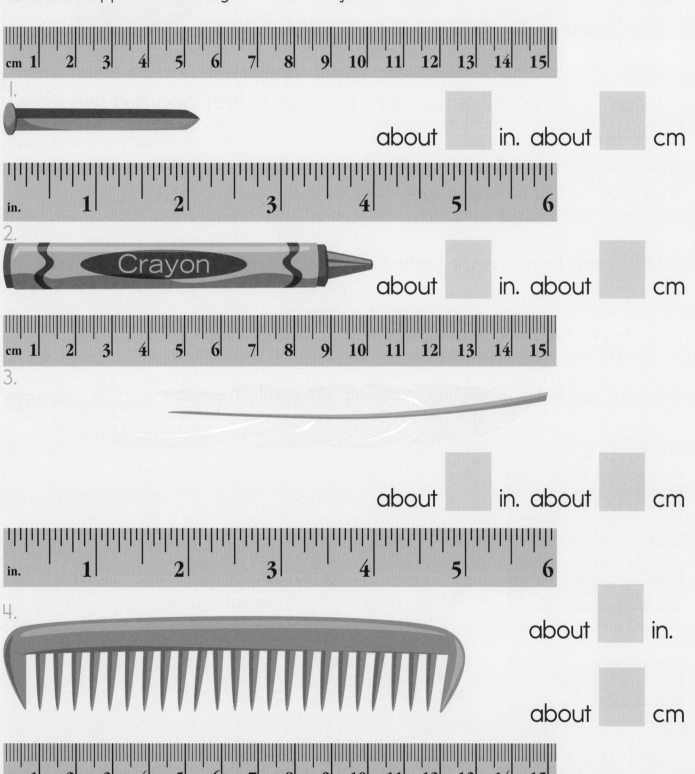

1.

about [ ] in. about [ ] cm

2. Crayon

about [ ] in. about [ ] cm

3.

about [ ] in. about [ ] cm

4.

about [ ] in.

about [ ] cm

Work It Out

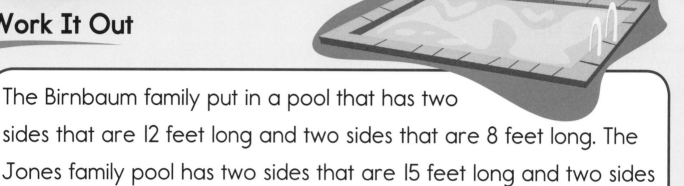

The Birnbaum family put in a pool that has two sides that are 12 feet long and two sides that are 8 feet long. The Jones family pool has two sides that are 15 feet long and two sides that are 7 feet long.

WRITE the perimeter of each pool, and CIRCLE the name of the family with the pool with the larger perimeter.

1. Birnbaum family: pool perimeter = ☐ feet

2. Jones family: pool perimeter = ☐ feet

Annie is trying to figure out how many rugs she can fit in her room. WRITE the area of the room and the tile. Then ANSWER the question.

Room:

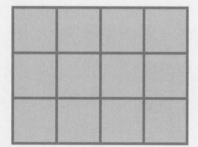

3. Room area:  square units

Rug:

4. Rug area: 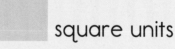 square units

5. What is the total number of rugs Annie will need to cover her floor?

Squared Away

WRITE the perimeter and area of each shape.

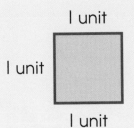

I unit

I unit | I unit

I unit

Perimeter: 4 units

Area: I square unit

1.

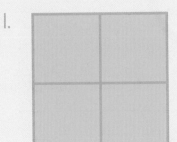

Perimeter: ___ units

Area: ___ square units

2.

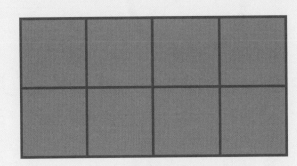

Perimeter: ___ units

Area: ___ square units

3.

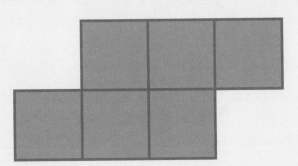

Perimeter: ___ units

Area: ___ square units

4.

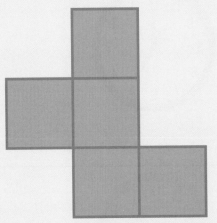

Perimeter: ___ units

Area: ___ square units

Hours & Half Hours

What Time Is It?

WRITE the time on each clock.

Examples:

4 : 00   8 : 30

1.

:

2.

:

3.

:

4.

:

5.

:

6.

:

Watch It!

DRAW a line to connect each watch to a clock that shows the same time.

Hours & Half Hours

Give Me a Hand

DRAW the clock hands to match the time.

1.

1:30

2.

4:00

3.

6:00

4.

8:30

5.

5:30

6.

3:00

7.

11:30

8.

7:30

Passing the Time

DRAW the time on the last clock to complete the pattern.

1.

2.

3.

4.

Quarter Hours

What Time Is It?

WRITE the time on each clock.

Examples:

 1 : 15

 5 : 45

1.

:

2.

:

3.

:

4.

:

5.

 :

6.

 :

Watch It!

DRAW a line to connect each watch to a clock that shows the same time.

Quarter Hours

Give Me a Hand

DRAW the clock hands to match the time.

1.

4:15

2.

12:45

3.

7:15

4.

1:45

5.

10:45

6.

5:15

7.

8:15

8.

2:45

Passing the Time

DRAW the time on the last clock to complete the pattern.

1.

2.

3.

4.

It's about Time

15-Minute Warning

Mom says you're leaving in 15 minutes. WRITE the time you need to go.

1.
 + 15 minutes = ☐ : ☐

2.
 + 15 minutes = ☐ : ☐

3.
 + 15 minutes = ☐ : ☐

4.
 + 15 minutes = ☐ : ☐

Set Your Clock

Each clock is slow. DRAW hands to show the correct time on each clock.

HINT: Add time to each clock.

1.

 2 hours slow ⟶

2.

 30 minutes slow ⟶

3.

 15 minutes slow ⟶

4.

 45 minutes slow ⟶

It's about Time

Set Your Clock

Each clock is fast. DRAW hands to show the correct time on each clock.

HINT: Subtract time from each clock.

1.

 15 minutes fast ⟶

2.

 3 hours fast ⟶

3.

 45 minutes fast ⟶

4.

 30 minutes fast ⟶

Time Difference

WRITE the difference in time between each pair of clocks.

1.

 hours   minutes

2.

 hours   minutes

3.

 hours   minutes

4.

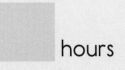 hours    minutes

Calendars

Save the Date

CIRCLE the correct answer.

Month

NOVEMBER						
S	M	T	W	T	F	S
	1	2	3	4	5	6
7	8	9	10	11	12	13
14	15	16	17	18	19	20
21	22	22	23	25	26	27
28	29	30				

Days of the week:
Sunday
Monday
Tuesday
Wednesday
Thursday
Friday
Saturday

1. What month is this?

   December   July   November

2. How many days are in this month?

   29   30   31

3. What is the first day of this month?

   Monday   Thursday   Saturday

4. What is the date of the first Friday?

   November 1   November 5   November 12

5. How many Mondays are in this month?

   3   4   5

6. How many Fridays are in this month?

   3   4   5

Save the Date

WRITE the correct answer.

JANUARY						
S	M	T	W	T	F	S
					1	2	3
4	5	6	7	8	9	10
11	12	13	14	15	16	17
18	19	20	21	22	23	24
25	26	27	28	29	30	31

FEBRUARY						
S	M	T	W	T	F	S
1	2	3	4	5	6	7
8	9	10	11	12	13	14
15	16	17	18	19	20	21
22	23	24	25	26	27	28

MARCH						
S	M	T	W	T	F	S
1	2	3	4	5	6	7
8	9	10	11	12	13	14
15	16	17	18	19	20	21
22	23	24	25	26	27	28
29	30	31

APRIL						
S	M	T	W	T	F	S
			1	2	3	4
5	6	7	8	9	10	11
12	13	14	15	16	17	18
19	20	21	22	23	24	25
26	27	28	29	30

MAY						
S	M	T	W	T	F	S
					1	2
3	4	5	6	7	8	9
10	11	12	13	14	15	16
17	18	19	20	21	22	23
24	25	26	27	28	29	30
31

JUNE						
S	M	T	W	T	F	S
	1	2	3	4	5	6
7	8	9	10	11	12	13
14	15	16	17	18	19	20
21	22	23	24	25	26	27
28	29	30

JULY						
S	M	T	W	T	F	S
			1	2	3	4
5	6	7	8	9	10	11
12	13	14	15	16	17	18
19	20	21	22	23	24	25
26	27	28	29	30	31

AUGUST						
S	M	T	W	T	F	S
						1
2	3	4	5	6	7	8
9	10	11	12	13	14	15
16	17	18	19	20	21	22
23	24	25	26	27	28	29
30	31

SEPTEMBER						
S	M	T	W	T	F	S
		1	2	3	4	5
6	7	8	9	10	11	12
13	14	15	16	17	18	19
20	21	22	23	24	25	26
27	28	29	30

OCTOBER						
S	M	T	W	T	F	S
				1	2	3
4	5	6	7	8	9	10
11	12	13	14	15	16	17
18	19	20	21	22	23	24
25	26	27	28	29	30	31

NOVEMBER						
S	M	T	W	T	F	S
1	2	3	4	5	6	7
8	9	10	11	12	13	14
15	16	17	18	19	20	21
22	23	24	25	26	27	28
29	30

DECEMBER						
S	M	T	W	T	F	S
		1	2	3	4	5
6	7	8	9	10	11	12
13	14	15	16	17	18	19
20	21	22	23	24	25	26
27	28	29	30	31

1. How many months are in one year? _____

2. What is the first month of the year? _____

3. Which month has 28 days? _____

4. How many months have 31 days? _____

5. What day of the week is Valentine's Day, February 14?

   _____

6. On what day of the week does October begin?

   _____

Save the Date

DRAW the pictures for the special events on the correct place on the calendar.

HINT: Some events last longer than one day.

Maya's beach party	July 17	☀
Florida vacation	July 30 to August 6	V
First day of school	August 31	1
Tyler's birthday	August 12	🎈
Mom and Dad's anniversary	July 29	💍
Dad and Tyler's fishing trip	August 21–22	🐟
Hota Dakota concert	July 3	♫
Dentist appointment	August 9	🦷

JULY

Sunday	Monday	Tuesday	Wednesday	Thursday	Friday	Saturday
				1	2	3
4	5	6	7	8	9	10
11	12	13	14	15	16	17
18	19	20	21	22	23	24
25	26	27	28	29	30	31

AUGUST

Sunday	Monday	Tuesday	Wednesday	Thursday	Friday	Saturday
1	2	3	4	5	6	7
8	9	10	11	12	13	14
15	16	17	18	19	20	21
22	23	24	25	26	27	28
29	30	31				

Review

What Time Is It?

WRITE the time on each clock.

1.

     ☐ : ☐

2.

     ☐ : ☐

3.

     ☐ : ☐

4.

     ☐ : ☐

5.

     ☐ : ☐

6.

     ☐ : ☐

7.

     ☐ : ☐

8.

     ☐ : ☐

Unit Rewind

WRITE the new time.

1.  + 45 minutes = ☐ : ☐

2. + 15 minutes = ☐ : ☐

3.  + 30 minutes = ☐ : ☐

4.  + 45 minutes = ☐ : ☐

APRIL						
S	M	T	W	T	F	S
					1	2
3	4	5	6	7	8	9
10	11	12	13	14	15	16
17	18	19	20	21	22	23
24	25	26	27	28	29	30

5. How many days are in this month? _____

6. On what day of the week does this month begin? _____

7. What is the date of the first Wednesday?

_____

8. What day of the week is April 26?

_____

Money Values

Which One?

CIRCLE the money that matches the dollar amount.

$1.42   

$0.80   

$1.23   

$1.86   

$2.06   

$5.55   

Match Up

DRAW lines to connect money with the same value.

Money Values

Money Bags

WRITE the value of the money on the bag.

1.

$ ___ . ___

2.

$ ___ . ___

3.

$ ___ . ___

4.

$ ___ . ___

5.

$ ___ . ___

6.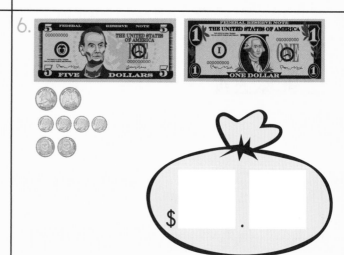

$ ___ . ___

Odd One Out

CROSS OUT the picture or number that does **not** match the others.

$0.70

$1.16

$3.62

$5.85

Pay Up

CIRCLE the money needed to buy each item using exact change.

$1.15

$2.39

$3.90

$5.53

$8.41

Match Up

DRAW lines to connect the money with the food that can be bought using exact change.

$2.74

$3.03

$1.99

$6.57

$2.66

Using Money

Who Can Buy It?

CIRCLE the hands of the people who have enough money to buy a movie ticket.

MONSTER MAYHEM
IN 3-D
$ 14.75

TICKETS

Pay Up

WRITE the cost to buy all three things.

$3.20

$9.68

$15.09

Total cost $ ___ . ___

Circle It

CIRCLE all of the objects that cost **less** than the top object.

$8.93

$9.37

$2.44

$10.50

$5.89

$4.16

Matched or Mismatched?

WRITE >, <, or = in each box.

1.

2.

3.

4.
$2.99

5.
$4.02

6.
$6.52

7.
$8.85

Money Bags

WRITE the value of the money on the bag.

1.

$ [   ] . [   ]

2.

$ [   ] . [   ]

3.

$ [   ] . [   ]

4.

$ [   ] . [   ]

5.

$ [   ] . [   ]

6.

$ [   ] . [   ]

Review

Pay Up

CIRCLE the money needed to buy the soccer ball using exact change.

$9.49

WRITE the cost to buy all three things.

$8.50

$2.30

$4.29

Total cost $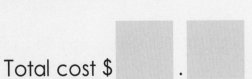

Which Is Less?

CIRCLE the picture with **less** money than the other.

Mismatched

WRITE > or < in each box.

1. $0.13 ☐ $0.56

2. $5.44 ☐ $4.30

3. $2.69 ☐ $2.07

4. $5.21 ☐ $5.18

5. $8.25 ☐ $9.77

6. $3.32 ☐ $3.20

Answers

Page 2
1. 53   2. 25
3. 39   4. 17
5. 72   6. 81
7. 46   8. 68

Page 3
1. 16   2. 49
3. 83   4. 75
5. 58   6. 32
7. 94   8. 67

Page 4
1. 182   2. 433
3. 925   4. 657
5. 708

Page 5

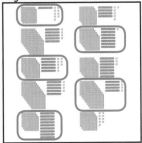

Page 6
1. one hundred sixty-two
2. three hundred seventy-four
3. two hundred fifty
4. eight hundred sixteen
5. six hundred forty-three
6. four hundred ninety-five

Page 7

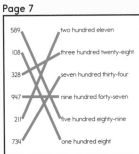

589 — five hundred eighty-nine
108 — one hundred eight
328 — three hundred twenty-eight
947 — nine hundred forty-seven
211 — two hundred eleven
734 — seven hundred thirty-four

Pages 8–9

1	2	3	4	5	6	7	8	9	10
11	12	13	14	15	16	17	18	19	20
21	22	23	24	25	26	27	28	29	30
31	32	33	34	35	36	37	38	39	40
41	42	43	44	45	46	47	48	49	50
51	52	53	54	55	56	57	58	59	60
61	62	63	64	65	66	67	68	69	70
71	72	73	74	75	76	77	78	79	80
81	82	83	84	85	86	87	88	89	90
91	92	93	94	95	96	97	98	99	100

Page 10

82	83	84	85	86	87	88	89

103	104	105	106	107	108	109	110

343	344	345	346	347	348	349	350

719	720	721	722	723	724	725	726

566	567	568	569	570	571	572	573

850	851	852	853	854	855	856	857

Page 11

234	235	236	237	238	239	240	241

981	982	983	984	985	986	987	988

97	98	99	100	101	102	103	104

874	875	876	877	878	879	880	881

699	700	701	702	703	704	705	706

395	396	397	398	399	400	401	402

Page 12

2	4	6	8	10	12	14	16

50	55	60	65	70	75	80	85

60	70	80	90	100	110	120	130

15	18	21	24	27	30	33	36

8	16	24	32	40	48	56	64

42	48	54	60	66	72	78	84

Page 13

66	68	70	72	74	76	78	80

20	30	40	50	60	70	80	90

15	20	25	30	35	40	45	50

27	30	33	36	39	42	45	48

62	66	70	74	78	82	86	90

42	49	56	63	70	77	84	91

Page 14

Page 15
1. 576   2. 329
3. 707   4. 458
5. 910

Page 16
1. <   2. >
3. <   4. >
5. <   6. <
7. >   8. <
9. >   10. >
11. >   12. <
13. <   14. >
15. <   16. >
17. <   18. >

Page 17
1. >   2. <
3. =   4. >
5. <   6. >
7. >   8. =

Page 18
1. 10   2. 20
3. 60   4. 70
5. 30   6. 40
7. 50   8. 60

Page 19
1. 700   2. 900
3. 400   4. 300
5. 500   6. 400
7. 200   8. 700
9. 300   10. 900
11. 700   12. 900

Page 20
Check:
1. 25
2. 160
3. 108

Page 21
Check:
1. 36
2. 17
3. 47

Page 22
1. 382, three hundred eighty-two
2. 740, seven hundred forty
3. 519, five hundred nineteen
4. 495, four hundred ninety-five
5. 906, nine hundred six

Page 23

245	246	247	248	249	250	251	252

589	590	591	592	593	594	595	596

724	725	726	727	728	729	730	731

40	45	50	55	60	65	70	75

26	29	32	35	38	41	44	47

11	17	23	29	35	41	47	53

Page 24
1. >   2. =
3. <   4. >
5. <   6. =
7. <   8. >
9. <

Page 25
1. 90   2. 30
3. 40   4. 60
5. 10   6. 100
7. 10   8. 20
9. 600   10. 200
11. 500   12. 700
13. 200   14. 400
15. 900   16. 200

17. Check: 58

Page 26
1. 56   2. 29
3. 78   4. 44
5. 68   6. 69

Page 27
1. 62   2. 96
3. 44   4. 89
5. 57   6. 79

Page 28
1. 79   2. 54
3. 98   4. 87
5. 44   6. 39
7. 76   8. 69
9. 77   10. 48
11. 31   12. 97
13. 59   14. 94
15. 64   16. 89

Page 29
1. 10   2. 21
3. 12   4. 45
5. 42   6. 65
7. 72   8. 18
9. 22   10. 13
11. 51   12. 43
13. 32   14. 31
15. 22   16. 12

Page 30
1. 43   2. 32
3. 52   4. 25
5. 13   6. 61

Page 31
1. 35   2. 31
3. 60   4. 12
5. 26   6. 41

Page 32
1. 27   2. 10
3. 21   4. 12
5. 81   6. 25
7. 62   8. 13
9. 40   10. 11
11. 30   12. 24
13. 52   14. 15
15. 72   16. 31

Answers

Page 33
1. 50 2. 46
3. 12 4. 15
5. 41 6. 20
7. 27 8. 21
9. 95 10. 34
11. 30 12. 69
13. 75 14. 24
15. 57 16. 48

Page 34
1. 42 2. 93
3. 82 4. 65
5. 91 6. 70

Page 35
1. 65 2. 92
3. 70 4. 81
5. 52 6. 73

Page 36
1. 61 2. 81
3. 90 4. 91
5. 70 6. 74
7. 35 8. 58
9. 32 10. 80
11. 66 12. 92

Page 37
1. 60 2. 75
3. 92 4. 67
5. 90 6. 41
7. 82 8. 50
9. 71 10. 64
11. 100 12. 95

Page 38
1. 67 2. 16
3. 39 4. 73
5. 18 6. 27

Page 39
1. 28 2. 18
3. 39 4. 66
5. 15 6. 57

Page 40
1. 59 2. 8
3. 29 4. 18
5. 38 6. 25
7. 26 8. 55
9. 37 10. 9
11. 28 12. 19

Page 41
1. 17 2. 4
3. 79 4. 57
5. 19 6. 38
7. 23 8. 41
9. 39 10. 47
11. 74 12. 9

Page 42
1. 22 2. 40
3. 45 4. 23
5. 56 6. 6

Page 43
1. 49
2. 44
3. 8
4. 12

Page 44
1. 61 2. 41
3. 20 4. 16
5. 79 6. 22
7. 44 8. 56
9. 89 10. 51
11. 15 12. 87

Page 45
1. 58 2. 39
3. 95 4. 89
5. 91 6. 81
7. 75 8. 64
9. 42 10. 33
11. 50 12. 21
13. 16 14. 14
15. 48 16. 29

Page 46
10

Page 47
8, 64

Page 48
1. 9 2. 6
3. 4 4. 3

Page 49
1. 4 2. 24
3. 12 4. 8

Page 50
1. 4
2. 6
3. 2

Page 51
4

Page 52
1. 3 2. 4
3. 7 4. 5

Page 53
1. 1, 2
2. 5, 3
3. 4, 2

Page 54
1. odd 2. even
3. odd 4. even
5. even 6. odd

Page 55
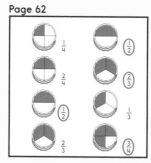

Page 56
1. 12 2. 8
3. 6 4. 4
5. 3

Page 57
1. 9 2. odd
3. even 4. odd

Page 58
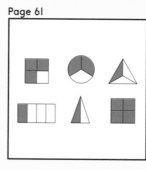

Page 59
1. $\frac{1}{4}$ 2. $\frac{1}{2}$ 3. $\frac{1}{3}$
4. $\frac{3}{4}$ 5. $\frac{3}{4}$ 6. $\frac{2}{3}$

Page 60
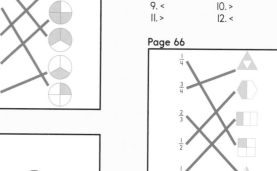

Page 61

Page 62

Page 63
1. $\frac{3}{4}$ $\left(\frac{1}{2}\right)$
2. $\left(\frac{2}{3}\right)$ $\frac{2}{2}$
3. $\frac{4}{4}$ $\left(\frac{2}{3}\right)$
4. $\frac{3}{4}$ $\left(\frac{2}{4}\right)$

Page 64
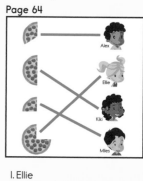

1. Ellie
2. Miles

Page 65
1. < 2. >
3. = 4. >
5. > 6. >
7. < 8. =
9. < 10. >
11. > 12. <

Page 66

Page 67

Page 68
1. 6
2. 3
3. 8
4. 4
5. 6
6. 2

Answers

Page 69
1. 7 2. 4
3. 3 4. 5
5. 6

Page 70
Check:
1. 7 2. 4
3. 9 4. 6
5. 8

Page 71
Ask someone to check your answers.

Page 72
1. 2 2. 5
3. 3 4. 1
5. 4 6. 3

Page 73
1. 5 2. 4
3. 7 4. 6

Page 74
Check:
1. 6 2. 3
3. 5 4. 2
5. 4

Page 75
Ask someone to check your answers.

Page 76
1. 4 2. 8
3. 5 4. 10
5. 2 6. 6

Page 77
1. 13 2. 11
3. 15 4. 12

Page 78
Check:
1. 7 2. 14
3. 8 4. 12
5. 16

Page 79
Ask someone to check your answers.

Page 80
1. 16 2. 12
3. 18 4. 11

Page 81

Perimeter: 39 cm

Page 82
1. 9 2. 8
3. 5 4. 5
5. 6 6. 10

Page 83

Page 84
1. Sarah
2. Jackie
3. Willa

Page 85
1. 2, 5 2. 4, 10
3. 6, 15 4. 5, 13

Page 86
1. 40
2. 44 [Jones circled]
3. 12
4. 2
5. 6

Page 87
1. 8, 4 2. 12, 8
3. 12, 6 4. 12, 5

Page 88
1. 1:30 2. 10:00
3. 5:00 4. 12:30
5. 2:30 6. 7:00

Page 89

Page 90

Page 91

Page 92
1. 3:45 2. 12:15
3. 10:15 4. 4:45
5. 8:45 6. 10:15

Page 93

Page 94

Page 95

Page 96
1. 2:15 2. 11:45
3. 4:00 4. 6:30

Page 97

Page 98

Page 99
1. 3 hours 30 minutes
2. 2 hours 15 minutes
3. 4 hours 30 minutes
4. 4 hours 15 minutes

Page 100
1. November
2. 30
3. Monday
4. November 5
5. 5
6. 4

Page 101
1. 12
2. January
3. February
4. 7
5. Saturday
6. Thursday

Pages 102–103

Page 104
1. 3:30 2. 12:15
3. 8:45 4. 4:00
5. 5:15 6. 2:45
7. 9:45 8. 6:30

Answers

Page 105
1. 12:45
2. 6:00
3. 8:00
4. 2:30
5. 30
6. Friday
7. April 6
8. Tuesday

Page 106

Page 107

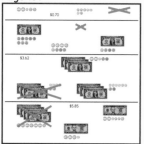

Page 108
1. $0.82   2. $1.41
3. $2.35   4. $2.11
5. $5.47   6. $7.00

Page 109

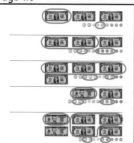

Page 110

Page 111

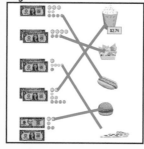

Page 112

Page 113
$27.97

Page 114

Page 115
1. >   2. <
3. =   4. <
5. >   6. <
7. =

Page 116
1. $1.71
2. $6.22
3. $5.20
4. $9.04
5. $10.98
6. $13.07

Page 117

$15.09

Page 118

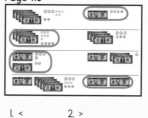

1. <   2. >
3. >   4. >
5. <   6. >